DARTINGTON HALL

One Endless Garden

Dedicated to the memory of Leonard and Dorothy Elmhirst

DARTINGTON HALL
One Endless Garden

the photographs of
CAROL BALLENGER

WITH QUOTES FROM DOROTHY ELMHIRST'S GARDEN NOTEBOOKS

HALSGROVE

First published in Great Britain in 2012

British Library Cataloguing-in-Publication Data
A CIP record for this title is available from the British Library

ISBN 978 0 85704 153 1

HALSGROVE
Halsgrove House,
Ryelands Business Park,
Bagley Road, Wellington, Somerset TA21 9PZ
Tel: 01823 653777   Fax: 01823 216796
email: sales@halsgrove.com

Part of the Halsgrove group of companies
Information on all Halsgrove titles is available at: www.halsgrove.com

Printed in China by Everbest Printing Co Ltd

LOTTERY FUNDED

Dartington

My thanks go to everyone who has helped during the making of this book, particularly family and friends including Graham Hodgson for help with sequencing the photographs, and John Powls for the use of his poetry.

I am deeply indebted to my publisher Simon Butler at Halsgrove for his encouragement and support from the earliest days when the book was just an idea, continuing through the many stages to bring it to fruition. Thanks also to designer Sharon O'Inn for her ideas, skill and patience in dealing with my many revisions.

There are a number of people associated with Dartington whose help I wish to acknowledge: Yvonne Widger at the Archives; the Gardens Committee; Satish Kumar and David Francis, Director of Arts. I especially thank Graham Gammin, Grounds and Gardens Manager, for providing plant names and helping me to a better understanding of the Gardens and, in addition, for kindly writing the Foreword.

I am grateful to the Dartington Hall Trust and Arts Council England for their financial support for *Arts Live* and the *Dartington Project* of which this book is one element. I also thank the Trust for the opportunity to photograph in this beautiful place and to be able to include in the book the so apt and poetic quotes from Dorothy Elmhirst's garden notebooks.

ACKNOWLEDGEMENTS

FOREWORD

The Gardens of Dartington Hall captivated me from the very first moment of discovery. Like so many local people, I knew of Dartington and the beautiful but secretive lower drive winding its way up the hill with glorious views of the Dart – a river I had canoed upon many times as a child – but I never knew what lay just beyond that mysterious archway entrance.

Later, I found out, and instantly fell under the spell of Dartington Hall Gardens; a spell that holds on to its victims, ever drawing them back. In 1979 I became head gardener and thirty-three years later I am still under its spell.

The Hall Gardens have a quiet strength about them, a quality that is so very hard to describe but so evident to those who are open to it. Others talk of 'magic' and the place has been described as a 'veritable fairyland'. These are not terms that come easily to a practical person like me, but there is presence; a vitality here that comes from the values and creativity of the generations who have gone before.

In the 1920s, when the Elmhirst's first discovered Dartington, it was in a ruinous state, but they understood the significance of place. Realising the potential, they had the vision and the means to evolve a new and modern garden, set within the powerful, historic heart of their ongoing experiment in rural regeneration. Their garden would respect and value the work of those who went before, cherishing both natural and historic features. Theirs was a policy of 'freeing' and 'enhancing' and 'adding', but never imposing or dominating.

A walk through the Gardens is never predictable. Of course the icons remain the same: the borders, the ancient and majestic trees, the sculptures, the old walls and enigmatic tiltyard with terraces. They will always welcome the visitor whilst

holding their own secrets and stories. A walk in the garden involves all the senses and those sensual combinations are never the same. There are the obvious seasonal, weekly and daily changes as all living things progress through their calendar year, but there are also subtle, fleeting, all too brief changes of light and shade, the smells after rain, a light breeze, the sounds of birds hiding among the boughs and a myriad others. All are sub-plots that tantalise and contribute towards the 'whole garden' experience.

Carol Ballenger is a true artist with an enviable talent for capturing those special transient moments within her photography: a leafy pattern on wet stone; a knotty root breaking the moss; or moody views floating above and beyond arable fields - all these capture the moment and hint at so much more. Likewise, the extracts from Dorothy Elmhirst's notebooks give glimpses of how she was touched by the landscape and the garden that she created and loved.

Graham A. Gammin
Grounds and Gardens Manager
Dartington, 2012

Garden time measured
In seasons and the passage
Of sun and moon.

John Powls

INTRODUCTION

Beauty is ours, ours a countryside like one endless garden, wrote Leonard Elmhirst in a letter to the Indian poet Rabindranath Tagore on the day in 1925 when Leonard and his new wife Dorothy took possession of Dartington Hall.

The photographs in this book are the result of many years exploring this inspiring landscape and, for me, reflect the ethos of the place as embraced by the Elmhirsts, the founders of the modern Dartington. Theirs was a vision celebrating a reverence for nature and self-expression through the arts.

In a magnificent setting just above the tidal reaches of the River Dart, Dartington Hall dates back to the 14th century and its landscapes have been used and shaped for generations. The Elmhirsts acquired a neglected estate. With considerable resources, they were able to put their ideas for social and rural regeneration into practice – an endeavour they called "The English Experiment". The arts were always central to the plans of the Elmhirsts, be they hosts to an international dance company or the local community.

Encouraged by Tagore, the Elmhirsts founded a school which aimed to provide for students an environment which encouraged an appreciation of nature and freedom of expression. The school was modelled on Tagore's school at Shantiniketan in India of which Tagore said: *Harmony with all things arouses a desire to seek our freedom, not in the man-made world but in the depth of the universe, and makes us offer our reverence to the divinity inherent in fire, water and trees. The forming of my school had its origin in the memory of that longing for freedom, the memory which seems to go beyond the skyline of my birth.*

As well as renovating the Hall and courtyard the Elmhirsts commissioned fine examples of modernist architecture to be built on the estate, most notably High Cross House, designed by American architect William Lescaze as a home for the headmaster of Dartington School.

Today Dartington Hall has over one million visitors each year, many coming for concerts, films, theatre, and events such as the International Summer School of Music, Ways With Words and Tagore Festivals, and ecology courses at Schumacher College. A glimpse of these varied aspects of Dartington can be seen on the pages of this introduction. However this book is primarily a celebration of the enduring quality of the landscapes of Dartington Hall.

I first came to Dartington from the US as a music student in 1963 and was awed by the beauty and history of this magical place. The College of Arts had been founded a few years earlier, building on a tradition of education at Dartington and this ethos underpinned my studies at the College.

I had grown up on a farm in the foothills of the Appalachian Mountains in South Carolina. Landscape became important to me as a child and I was at my happiest when we visited the mountains or walked in the woods. I received my first camera at the age of ten, inspired by my mother who, for a number of years, took great delight in photographing the roses she grew. I photographed everything as often

as the cost of film would allow and remember the joy of collecting my developed prints from the "Jack Rabbit" photo shop.

As a student at Dartington the ideas I formed about music as a means of expression were later to inform my work as a photographer, although the links were not immediately obvious.

I continued my studies at the Royal College of Music in London and later renewed my interest in photography alongside working as a violinist for the Royal Ballet Orchestra. I regularly visited museums and galleries and was particularly drawn to and inspired by landscape artists such as Constable, Blake, Palmer and particularly the Americans Georgia O'Keeffe and Mark Rothko.

In 1975 I saw at the V & A an exhibition curated by British photographer Bill Brandt which changed my life - *The Land: 20th Century Landscape Photographs*. This featured the work of the modern American photographers including Alfred Steiglitz, Edward Weston and Ansel Adams along with Parisians Lartigue and Brassai, amongst others. I was stunned by the beauty and quality of these original prints and realised what a powerful medium of expression photography could be. I knew I wanted to become a photographer, and soon set up my first darkroom.

My first project, *Beyond the Great Wall*, documented a visit to China as a violinist with the English National Ballet. This was early 1979, just a few months after

diplomatic relations were resumed with the western world, and we were some of the first visitors to go to Beijing and Shanghai. Seen in the context of China today, my photographs documented the end of an era.

In 1980 I returned to Devon and soon became drawn to photograph Dartmoor. Here I could put into practice all the inspiration and techniques I had gleaned from reading, particularly the books of Ansel Adams. I love walking and spent many hours on the moor in all seasons observing its dramatic moods and changes of light. On the moor one is confronted with vast open spaces and I wanted to find a way of representing what I saw. Upon seeing an exhibition of the work of the Dartmoor landscape painter F J Widgery, I noted his use of granite landmarks (tors, standing stones and bridges) in his paintings and incorporated these ideas into my early images of the moor.

Over the next few years I was fortunate to attend workshops and get to know the work of some important landscape photographers working in the UK: Paul Hill, Thomas Joshua Cooper, John Blakemore and Fay Godwin with whom I kept in touch until her death in 2005. Through meeting Thomas Joshua Cooper, I came to appreciate how photographs can have multiple layers of meaning and a depth of expression capable of being interpreted in different ways by the viewer. He spoke of the importance of taking time, just gazing and finding the place where one could feel a relationship with the landscape and its historical connections. As Henry David Thoreau commented in his journal, *The question is not what you look at, but what you see.*

The techniques of photography have changed greatly since my early days of using film and working in the darkroom – however the skill, joy and art of making a meaningful photograph have not. Making darkroom prints gave me an understanding of working with contrast and texture which I feel has helped with my digital work. Digital techniques have opened up so many new ways of expressing ideas through photography. I am not particularly concerned how a photograph is made, but I *am* interested in what a photograph has to say.

In 1992, for the National Trust, I had my first exhibition which included some black and white prints of Dartington – a celebration of their Year of Landscape. This was followed shortly by a showing of my Dartmoor work for The National Park Authority. It was through this event that I met poet John Powls which resulted in *Dartmoor Dreams,* a book of photographs and poems. Continuing our collaboration we formed *Arts Live* and began to present live performances combining photography, music and poetry. It is a great pleasure for me to be involved as a musician as well showing images at these ongoing events.

In the late 1990s, influenced by the American photographer William Eggleston, I began working in colour, first in the urban environment (*The Red Comet*), subsequently returning to Dartmoor, with *Stone Universe* being published by Halsgrove in 2001. Here I developed a style which continues in my later work – moving in and photographing the details of landscape and placing these images into context by showing them alongside panoramas covering 180°, made possible by digital techniques.

In 2005 I was invited to photograph Japanese gardens in the UK, including the Zen Garden designed by Phillip Booth at Dartington. The exhibition titled *Ashide, A Second Nature*, with haiku poetry by John Powls, was first shown at the Japanese Embassy in London in 2006. Making these images presented a challenge. Having worked mostly in the natural environment, I was now faced with designed gardens – each a work of art in its own right. I wanted to convey the essence of these places in my own style and in a non-documentary way whilst being true to my subject. I became drawn to these gardens and over months I became aware of their qualities of stillness and reverence for nature.

I continued photographing Dartington in 2007, wanting to celebrate this special garden and its setting by the river Dart. Several times each week I walked to Dartington in all weathers and light, often waiting or returning another day for the right conditions to make a particular image, for example *Ghond in the Moonlight* and the panoramas *Reclining Figure in Snow* and *The Courtyard and Cherry Trees*.

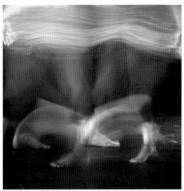

The Gardens form an essential part of the estate and it is these that feature predominantly in this book. Leonard Elmhirst upon first seeing Dartington Hall in March 1925, immediately realised its potential and wrote to Dorothy who was in New York: *We turned south on down the valley of the Dart to find Dartington Hall. We crept along a little cutting and came to a thatched lodge and gate with a bridge over a bubbling brooklet. In we went and up and down some wonderful hills, until we pulled up at a veritable fairyland – in winter too. What it would be like in spring or summer or autumn I dare not imagine.*

When Leonard and Dorothy Elmhirst first started their rural experiment they wanted to create a personal garden that could be shared with others. They worked with designers such as H Avray Tipping, Beatrix Farrand and Percy Cane. Dorothy Elmhirst was directly involved with the making of the gardens and her vision and passion are evident from reading her extensive garden notebooks which she kept from 1943 to 1968. I was privileged to be able to study these books in the Dartington Archives at High Cross House and soon realised that Dorothy Elmhirst's words had the simplicity and beauty that made them so appropriate for this book.

Dartington Hall and Gardens lie amongst woodlands and fields and these areas beyond the gardens have their place in this book. In the woods there are remains of medieval earthworks enclosing a deer park overlooking the river. In the stillness of the woods I am reminded of a quote by Rabindranath Tagore: *It seems that the subconscious remembrance of some primeval dwelling place, where our ancestors' minds were figured and voiced the mysteries of the inarticulate rocks, the rushing water and the dark whispers of the forest, was constantly stirring my blood with its call.*

In selecting the photographs for this book, it was a pleasure to be drawn back to the times of making each image. It is the mood, mystery and magic of a particular moment in my relationship with this place that is the essence of each photograph and I hope these qualities along with Dorothy Elmhirst's quotes have a resonance for those who read this book.

Carol Ballenger, 2012

Mood and landscape,
Defining times of peace
When even our own noise
Stills
For a moment.

John Powls

GARDENS

Spring walk is an absolute dream – it seems quite perfect to me.

*The two perfect days that always come sometime – warm and still –
and full of sun and shade and exquisite soft colour.*

The sun warms the earth and makes the birds to sing
and the heart of man to rejoice.

The cherries are like something entirely outside of previous experience. Seen over the yew hedge they look like snow peaks emerging out of dark forests in Switzerland.

The small group of fritillaries in the rock garden seems more fascinating than ever. We must have more.

This is the moment for the painter's palette – the gradations of green will escape even Jerry's coloured photos.

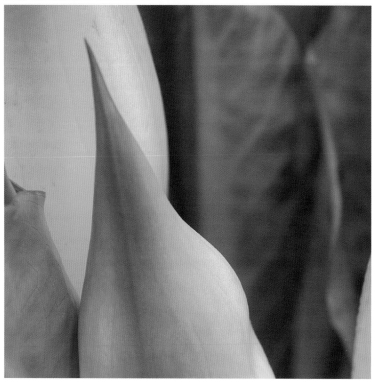

This is the high watermark of Spring beauty, with the beeches just emerging into that indescribably fresh green – and the oaks so ochrey, and the red acer the perfect foil for all the greens.

The smell of wisteria fills my room
at night – so strong it is that I feel
it must be in a vase beside me.

*Jerry and I walked out through the grounds this morning –
and were speechless with the beauty of it all.*

Rain at last – the refreshment shines
everywhere. Suddenly all the
bluebells have appeared.

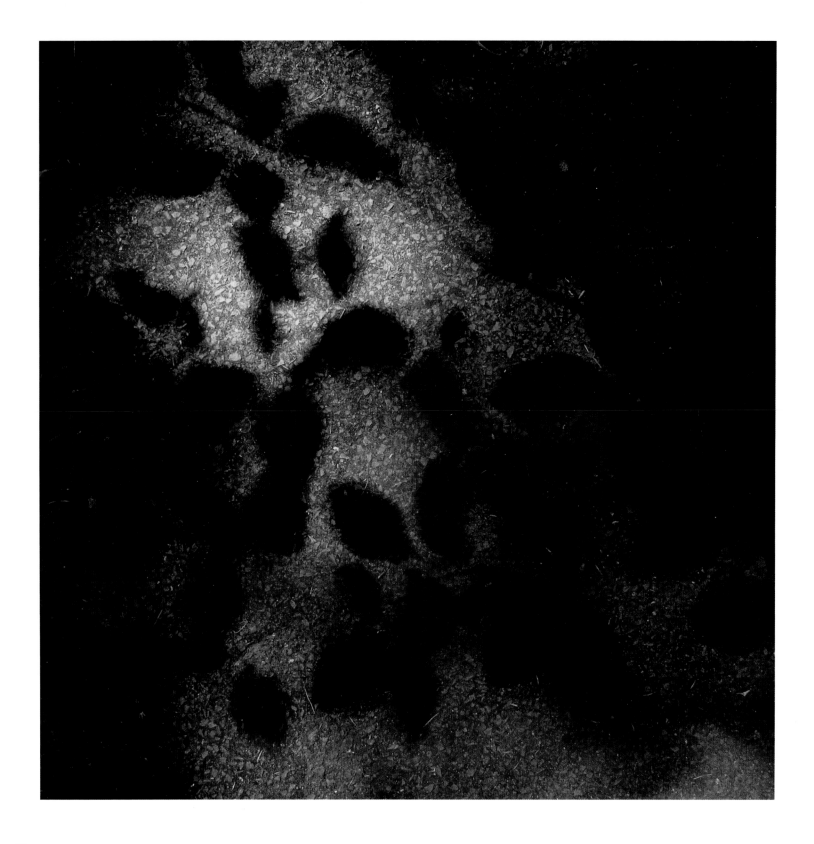

40

Garden open to the public. A better day – it is heavenly –
all of it – I feel so happy about the garden at last.

One of those breathlessly beautiful Sunday mornings
when the whole world seems at peace.

The most perfect of days – warm as midsummer –
mown grass, birds and my large garden hat.
Everything soaked in sunshine that burns.

A marvellous month of warm sunny days – we shall soon be complaining of drought.

Two really warm days –
tea out of doors –
cotton dress on – Joyful!

I realized today that it is shadows
which add so much to the beauty of everything.

A glowing warm day. Worked on Sunny Border.

The colours are such a rich gold everywhere and the oaks that deeper
russet that I dearly love. It is the moment for the cherries and the
oaks and the liquidambar – oh so heavenly.

Liquidambar now at its best –
so strange to find darkest
leaves at the top and some
of the palest down at the bottom.
The gradation is extraordinary.

Reluctantly, I watch leaves being swept
away from terraces and upper drive.

The moment when flame-coloured leaves of the chestnuts lie along the upper terrace like a shining carpet – reflecting light and colour – extraordinary glowing effect.

The beeches glow with the sun on them – burnt orange.
They are so wonderful the beeches.

*In the stillness the leaves of the beaches were fluttering down – like a game
I used to play with Jane trying to catch these evasive leaves as they fell.*

The incredible experience is to walk on the upper drive which is entirely covered by orange beech leaves – too much glory.

Raindrops hanging along small branches
like tiny silver bells.

Wet –
wetness everywhere –
two months of rain –
but some lovely
things to see.

*These moonlight nights have been
quite unearthly – absolute stillness.
Mild softness in the air.*

Jerry says the rain is no doubt helping "autumn growth".

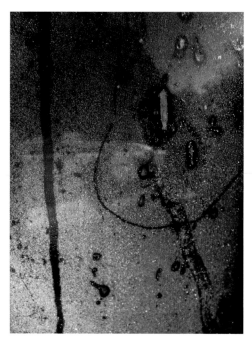  

Have cleared Sunny Border – very tidy – put away for winter.

Jerry home again! Walked in
the garden last night, and
this morning in soft rain.

*Anything to do with the garden
is absolute heaven to me.*

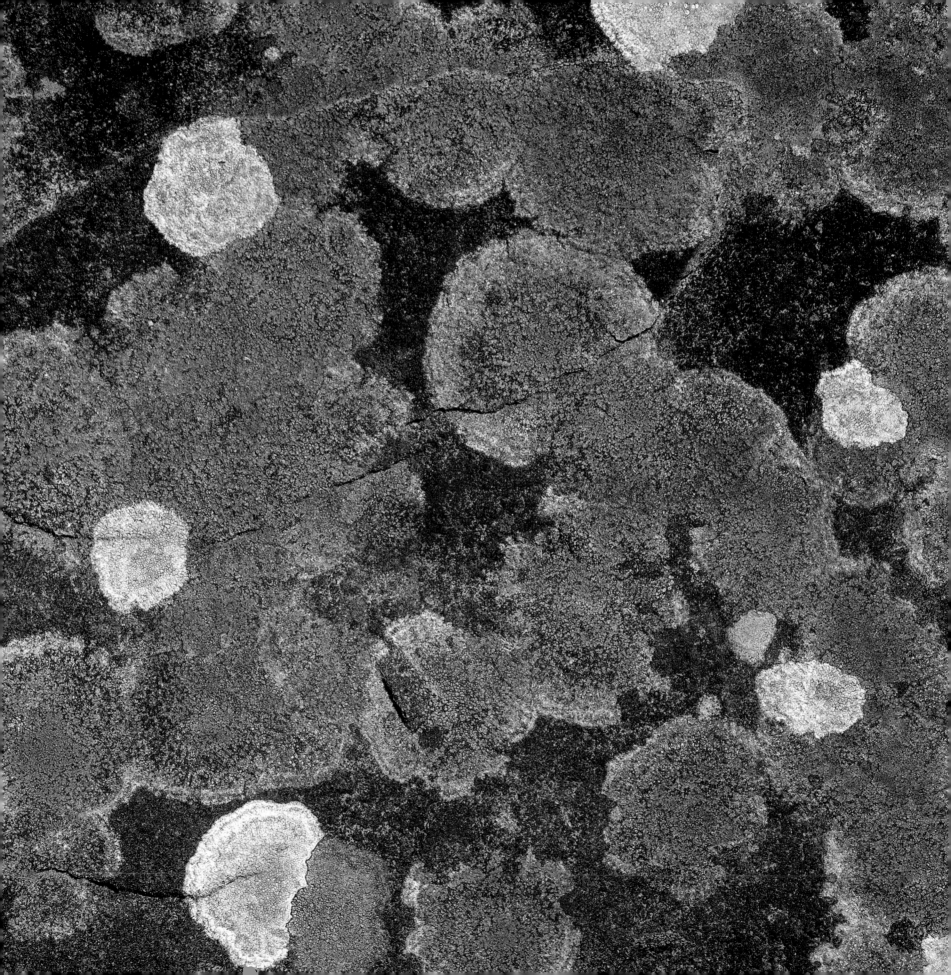

Returned from London at 2am in the midst of an American blizzard.
Today in walking about the snow came above my wellingtons.

A disaster has befallen Ghond – two days ago Mr Johnson noticed
a crack in the trunk, then last night, on Christmas eve, about 11pm –
Jerry and I from the study – heard the fatal sound of its fall.
Despite rain, Jerry went out with a lantern and found half
the tree gone – fallen back against the bank.
The front part is still strong and firm – but the other half – over
the terrace side – has split off and fallen – no harm done.
These trees seem to know how to fall with the least damage to others,
but... it is crushing to lose so much of our noble Ghond.

Four days of deep snow –
food brought up by sledge –
no cars, no buses.

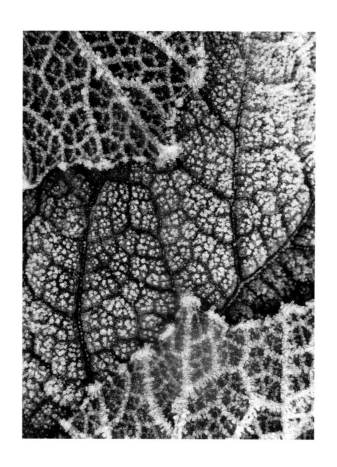

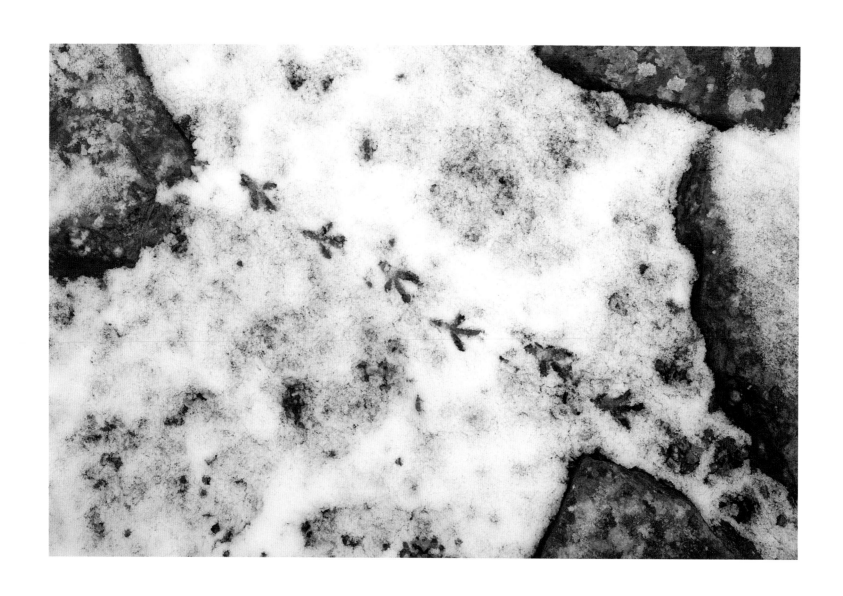

We've been feeding the birds – would we could do the
same for our tender trees and shrubs.

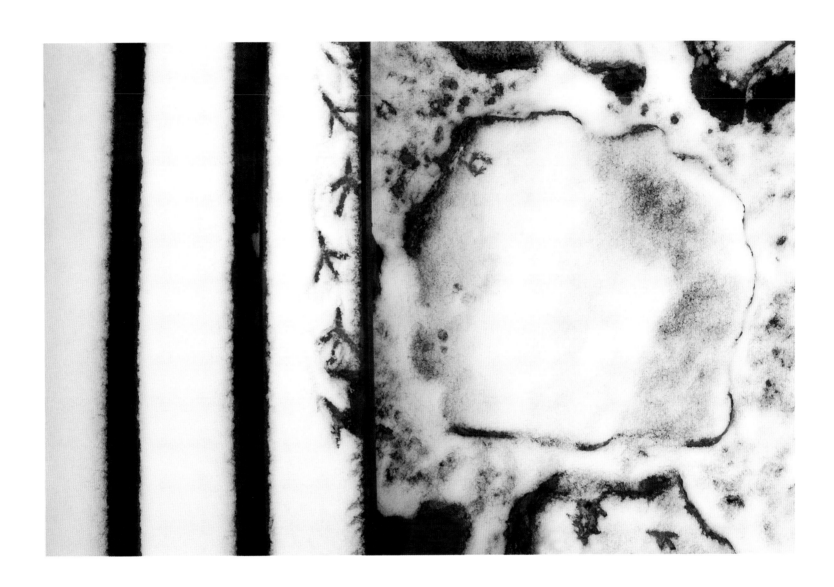

Today – at last – there has been some sun and a slight rise in temperature.
It is incredible what a difference the sun can make.

*At last and suddenly the weather has changed – the wind
is from the West, the sun is shining – there are shadows
again on the lawn, the birds are singing, the sky is blue,
the earth is soft and yielding. What an ecstacy it brings
to our frozen hearts.*

The wind has changed –
the softness of spring is in the air –
birds are singing and
peace is over all.

FIELDS

High Meadow has been cut down and forked over –
looks like a chocolate carpet.

*Last night I walked up over the hill above High Cross
and watched sunset over the blue moor hills.*

We've had nearly four weeks now of icy weather. It is so cold that one feels the whole world is held in a vice, paralized, immobile.

WOODS

The maroon tone of the alders against the deep blue of the river by Staverton Bridge.

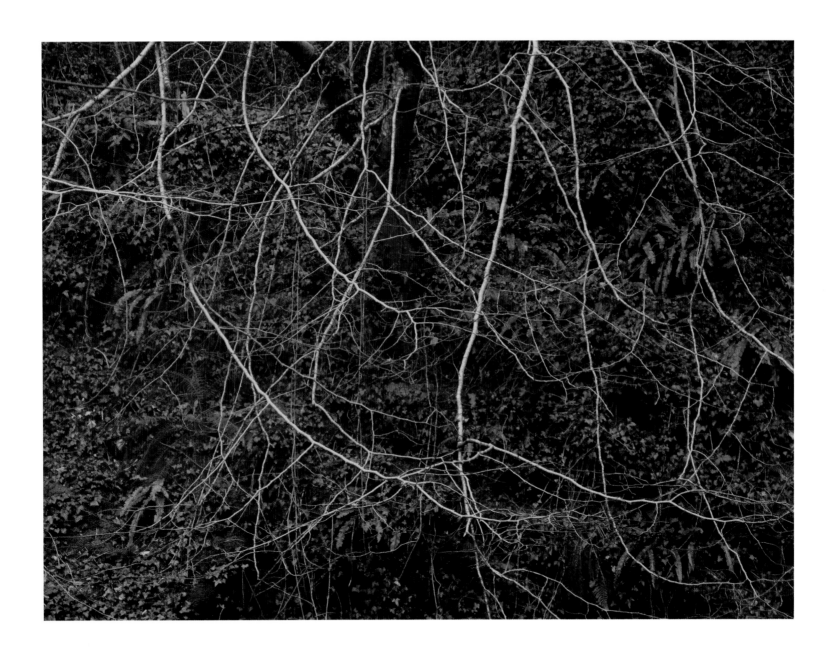

One of the perfect days full of stillness and sunshine.

*After three days in the house
I've had a walk! There's a
breathless stillness everywhere
and the silence seems to intensify
the colour of the beeches.*

Nature is our greatest source of beauty.

The stillness brings such peace.

139

Beauty is Ours

Just now all will be green at your door,
But not as green as Devon.
So I write to celebrate a day which must be memorable
In that we have taken possession of Dartington Hall today.
Beauty is ours -
Ours a countryside like one endless garden.
Can we find our true selves
And release those stores of creative vitality within us,
That uniting with other streamlets
All will flow like one river of silver life
Across a thirsty land?
We shall try. Dream for us.

Leonard Elmhirst writing to Tagore

What a revelation is here – of beauty, of variety,
of interest that never ceases to draw me into
the mystery of this wonderful place.

Dorothy Elmhirst

EPILOGUE

NOTES

57:     *The Glade* in autumn - Liquidambar leaves

61:     Fagus sylvatica (Beech)
        - tree since felled

67:     The *Swan Fountain* (1950)
        - made from Cornish granite by Willi Soukop, who also made the
        bronze *Donkey*

68:     Taxus baccata (Yew)
        - the oldest tree in the gardens, estimated to be 1500 - 2000 years old

73:     Pinus radiata (Monterey Pine)
         - *Ghond* (the Elmhirsts' name for the tree), in the moonlight

74:     Erigeron mucronatus (Crazy Daisy)

75:     *Jacobs Pillow* (2005) by Peter Randall Page

78:     Condensation on the Elmhirst children's playhouse windows

85:     Davidia involucrata vilmoriniana

89:     Castanea sativa (Sweet Chestnut)

91:     Pinus radiata (Monterey Pine)
        - *Ghond* was the name given by the Elmhirsts to this old tree

94:     Fagus sylvatica (Beech)

97:     *The Twelve Apostles* - (date from circa 1840s) Taxus baccata fastigiata
        (Irish Yews)

99:     *Japanese garden (1990)* designed by Philip Booth
        - an example of a Karesansui meditation garden

105:    Fagus sylvatica (Beech)

106:    Hamamelis x intermedia 'Pallida' (Witch Hazel)